Saturn's Secrets

Contents

Written by Rachael Davis

Collins

Spotting Saturn

We can gaze up at night and see planets.

Saturn

Jupiter

Saturn can be seen without a **telescope**.

Now, we can investigate, getting a closer look at Saturn, using robots and **probes**.

The first probe
flew by Saturn
in 1979.

Saturn up close

Saturn is the second biggest planet to **orbit** our Sun. It is made up of gases.

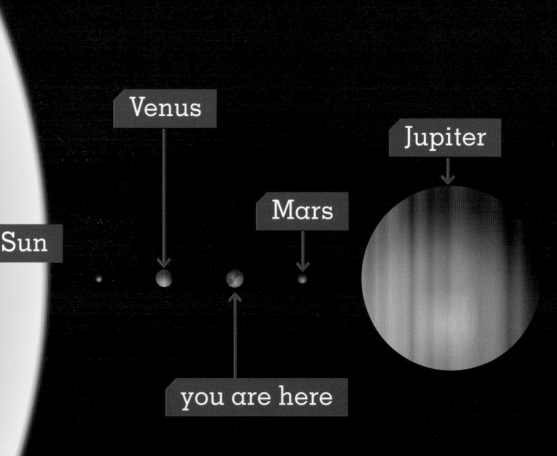

Sun

Venus

Mars

Jupiter

you are here

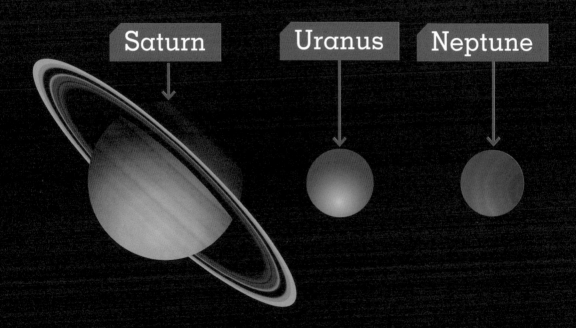

Saturn

Uranus

Neptune

Saturn has seven sets of rings surrounding it. There could be up to a thousand rings in all!

Each wide, thin ring consists of rock and frozen liquid.

Time on Saturn

Planets turn on their **axis**. One complete turn is a day.

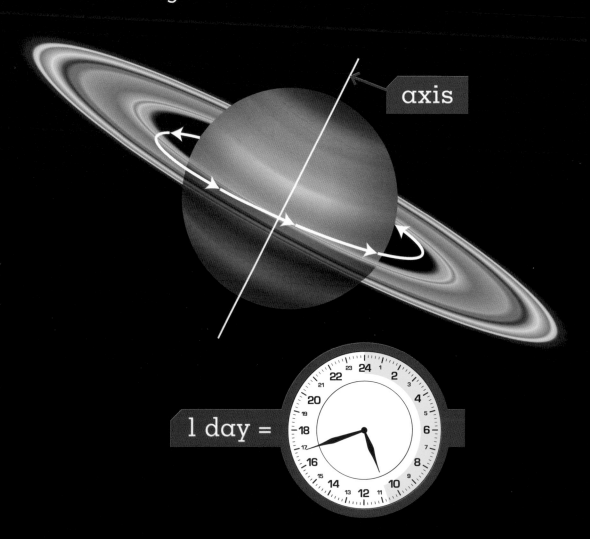

axis

1 day =

Days on our planet are longer than on Saturn.

axis

1 day =

Sun

you are here

orbit

One year on Saturn is the same as 29 years for us.

Saturn

Saturn's moons

Astronomers have identified that Saturn has at least 53 moons. Some have Greek names.

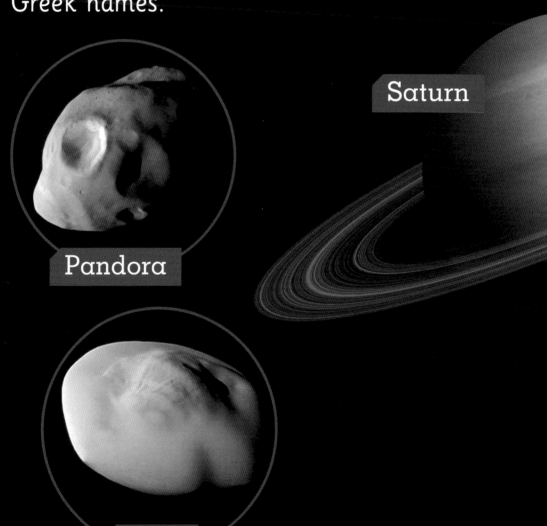

Saturn

Pandora

Atlas

Some are odd shapes and sizes. Janus is a potato-shaped moon!

Janus

Pan

Titan

Titan is Saturn's biggest moon and is the same size as a little planet!

Titan

Titan has clouds, rain, rivers and even lakes.

clouds

lakes

Life on Titan?

Saturn cannot support life, but some astronomers think Titan could.

astronomers experts on stars
and planets

axis a made-up line that a planet
turns around

orbit an object's track around
a planet, star or moon

probe a robot sent to investigate
a planet

telescope a long lens that makes
distant objects look closer

Index

Investigating Saturn

Review: After reading

Use your assessment from hearing the children read to choose any GPCs, words or tricky words that need additional practice.

Read 1: Decoding

- Ask the children to find words with these long vowel sounds on pages 6 and 7.
  On pages 6 and 7: /ai/ **made**   /oa/ **close**   /yoo/ **Neptune, Uranus**
                   /oo/ **Jupiter**   /ee/ **Venus**

- Challenge the children to read the glossary definitions. Say: Can you blend in your head when you read these words?

Read 2: Prosody

- Model reading pages 8 and 9 to the children as if you are presenting a science documentary.
- Ask the children to read the pages too, reminding them of ways they can make the information exciting and draw the viewer in:
  - Read the fact on page 8 with a surprised tone.
  - On page 9, experiment with emphasising words such as **each** and **and**.

Read 3: Comprehension

- Ask the children what they already know about Saturn or any of the other planets. Do they have a favourite planet, and if so, why?
- Discuss the title, and what they think the most interesting secret is. Ask: Which bit of information did you find the most interesting or surprising?
- Challenge the children to skim and scan the pages, using the contents and glossary too, to answer these questions.
  - How many moons does Saturn have? (*page 14: 53*)
  - Which moon might support life? (*page 18: Titan*)
  - What is an axis? (*page 20: a line that a thing turns around*)
- Look together at pages 22 and 23. Encourage the children to look at the pictures and recall some of the information they have learnt about Saturn and its moons.